THE WOJ

CW01022300

Three thousand yea[...]
there was a town c[...]
the Latin tribe – the ancestors o[...]
to Roman legend, its founder was Ascanius, son of the
fabled Aeneas of Troy. And so began an epic story that
started in a community of thatched huts and climaxed in
an empire encompassing millions of people across Europe,
North Africa and western Asia.

The power of Rome was at its peak between about
AD 100 and AD 120, and lasted until AD 476, when it
'fell'. Its influence lived on – especially in Byzantium
(Constantinople) in the East and through the Roman
Catholic Church and the Holy Roman Empire in the West.
In every land they conquered, including much of Britain,
the Romans left a rich legacy of attitudes and styles in
government, civic life, morality, technology and the arts –
and Roman ways coloured much of civilized life in Europe.
This book offers a glimpse into the remarkable history of
Rome and its empire, and will leave the reader, like a
spectator watching the entertainments in the Roman
arena, eager for more.

*A monumental stare: the outsize
head of Emperor Constantine, from
his fragmented statue in Rome.*

*Centre of power: Rome was the
hub of the Roman Empire. The
Colosseum (background) was
more theatre of nightmares
than stadium of light.*

*The Romans were not without
a sense of humour. These cupids
playing at being gladiators decorate
the Roman villa at Bignor in
West Sussex.*

THE RISE OF ROME

The people of Alba Longa were herders of sheep and cattle. Their immediate neighbours, Sabines, Volsci and others, were similarly pastoral. To the north was the empire of the Etruscans, sea-wanderers turned city-dwellers, an artistic people preoccupied with death and the underworld. In the south and west of Italy were sunnier minded Greeks, in colonies such as Cumae on the Bay of Naples, Syracuse in Sicily and Tarentum in the far south of Italy. Etruscans and Greeks were to have a profound influence on Rome.

By tradition, Romulus was born in Alba Longa and, with his brother Remus, founded Rome in 753 BC. Romulus built a wall to enclose the new settlement and became so incensed when his brother Remus mockingly jumped over it that he killed him, declaring that the same fate would befall anyone else who tried to cross the walls of Rome.

Archaeology seems to confirm that by the 8th century BC a community of farmers and herders was living on seven hills overlooking the River Tiber. They prospered and took up soldiering, but were not strong enough to fight off the Etruscans who, by 600 BC, had become their masters. The Etruscans built Rome's first temples and public buildings. In 509 BC, however, the Romans revolted and expelled Tarquin the Proud, the last of the seven legendary kings of Rome.

Rome was built by toil and conquest. Roman soldiers won the Empire and were energetic builders of its defences, as here, to keep out 'barbarians'. This relief is a copy from Trajan's Column, which records the Roman army at war.

Free from subjection, the Romans declared a republic. The Senate, an elected assembly, was controlled by a few noble families, the patricians, with whom the lower orders, or plebeians, engaged in a long struggle for power. As their military might grew, the Romans fought states that challenged them and eventually even the Etruscans were defeated. In the 400s BC, marauding Gauls (Celts from the north) captured Rome, but they were repulsed. In 280 BC, Pyrrhus of Epirus landed with 25,000 Greek troops and 20 war elephants, but they found the Romans too tough to crack. By 250 BC, Rome ruled all of Italy and the basis of Roman society had been established.

The she-wolf suckling Romulus and Remus. The infants were added to the original Etruscan-era bronze wolf in the 15th century.

THE MYTH OF ROMULUS AND REMUS

Romulus and Remus were the twin sons of Rhea Silvia, a princess of Alba Longa and a Vestal Virgin, who broke her vow of chastity with the god Mars. The babies were consigned to the River Tiber by Rhea Silvia's wicked uncle Amulius, who had seized the throne from her father Numitor. But the twins floated to land at the site of the future Rome. A she-wolf suckled the infants and they were raised to manhood by the herdsman Faustulus. The twins killed their great-uncle, restored their grandfather as king and founded Rome.

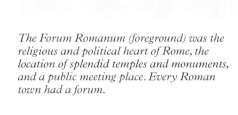

The Forum Romanum (foreground) was the religious and political heart of Rome, the location of splendid temples and monuments, and a public meeting place. Every Roman town had a forum.

REPUBLICAN RIGOURS

As a new Mediterranean force, Rome came into conflict with Carthage, the powerful Punic trading city in North Africa. After three Punic Wars, the Romans emerged triumphant, despite the prowess of the Carthaginian general, Hannibal (247–182 BC). Hannibal's defeat in 202 BC effectively meant the end for Carthage and the beginning of Rome's domination of Spain and North Africa. Rome also expanded eastwards, conquering Greece and Macedonia by the 140s BC.

The republic was fearful of both democracy and kingship: senators were deeply suspicious of any one man seizing supreme power. But the Senate was vulnerable to an ambitious man, who had soldiers to back him.

Hannibal of Carthage led an army of 40,000, with elephants, across the Pyrenees and Alps to invade Italy. His victory at Lake Trasimene (217 BC) dealt Rome one of its most disastrous defeats. The Romans hit back savagely and the Carthaginian general ended his life in exile.

Remains of the Roman baths at Carthage, Tunisia. By defeating Carthage, Rome achieved mastery over the Mediterranean.

Julius Caesar was born between 102 BC and 100 BC into one of Rome's leading families: he claimed to be a descendant of Aeneas of Troy and therefore from the goddess Venus, Aeneas's mother. He earned his laurels in the army, fighting in the East and in Spain, and was consul in 60 BC. In 58 BC he conquered much of Gaul; in 55 and 54 BC he campaigned in Britain. In 49 BC, with an army behind him, he crossed the Rubicon River to re-enter Italy, a move that sparked civil war. His victories alarmed the Senate, which ordered the veteran general Pompey to quash the upstart. Pompey tried, but was defeated at Pharsalus in 48 BC, and fled to Egypt, where he was murdered. Following Pompey to Egypt, Caesar (whose love life was the subject of much chit-chat in Rome) had an affair with Queen Cleopatra.

Back in Rome, Caesar declared himself 'dictator for life'. Alarmed, a group of high-placed Romans staged a coup. Caesar had once said he wanted a sudden death: he was stabbed 23 times on 15th March 44 BC.

Caesar's assassination did not save the republic. His adopted son Octavian and his former lieutenant Mark Antony went to war against the conspirators. After their victory at Philippi in 42 BC, they ruled the Roman world: Octavian in Rome and Mark Antony in Egypt, where like Caesar he became enamoured of Cleopatra.

PRIVATE ENTERPRISE

As a young man, Caesar was captured by pirates on his way to Rhodes. He raised his own ransom, then pursued the pirates with his private fleet. After rounding up his captors, he crucified them. A year or so later, he led a private army against King Mithradates of Pontus on the south shore of the Black Sea in what is now Turkey. He later used such incidents to justify toppling a government unable to protect its own citizens.

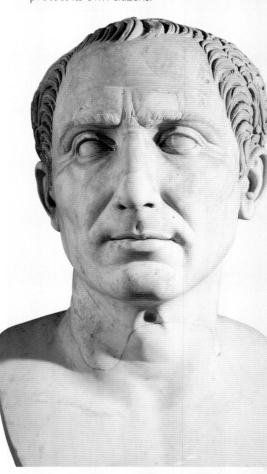

Julius Caesar was Rome's most successful general. His ambition alarmed his enemies in the Senate.

A relief showing a butcher's shop. While generals and politicians contested for power, ordinary Romans went about their business, seldom caring whether they lived in a republic or an empire.

IMPERIAL ROME

The Senate would not accept a divided Rome and Octavian was only too keen to get rid of Mark Antony. In 31 BC, Octavian's naval victory over Antony and Cleopatra at Actium won him sole control and reinforced Roman rigour over Eastern luxury. Both Cleopatra and Antony chose death rather than humiliation as captives.

In 27 BC, Octavian was awarded the title Augustus ('majestic'). He became the first Roman emperor. He rebuilt temples and, to restore moral standards in his role as 'first citizen' and 'father of the country', he encouraged the recreation of national myths. Virgil's epic poem, the *Aeneid*, extolled the greatness of Rome and the Augustan Age, Livy wrote a history of Rome in 142 books, and a period of peace and stability was ushered in.

The Baths of Caracalla in Rome, shown here in a 19th-century reconstruction, were big enough for 1,600 bathers. Emperor Caracalla (reigned AD 211– 217) was one of the more bloodthirsty emperors, likened by his enemies to a particularly ugly gladiator.

Emperor Augustus, in toga-draped marble dignity. A single-minded administrative genius, Augustus established the 'pax Romana' (Roman peace), and was deified after his death in AD 14.

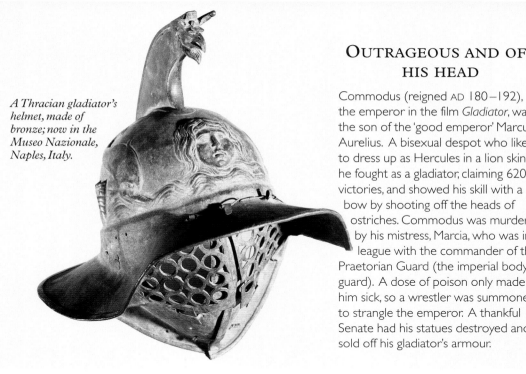

A Thracian gladiator's helmet, made of bronze; now in the Museo Nazionale, Naples, Italy.

OUTRAGEOUS AND OFF HIS HEAD

Commodus (reigned AD 180–192), the emperor in the film *Gladiator*, was the son of the 'good emperor' Marcus Aurelius. A bisexual despot who liked to dress up as Hercules in a lion skin, he fought as a gladiator, claiming 620 victories, and showed his skill with a bow by shooting off the heads of ostriches. Commodus was murdered by his mistress, Marcia, who was in league with the commander of the Praetorian Guard (the imperial body-guard). A dose of poison only made him sick, so a wrestler was summoned to strangle the emperor. A thankful Senate had his statues destroyed and sold off his gladiator's armour.

Augustus died in AD 14. His successors were a very mixed bunch and their reigns the stuff of racy novels and television dramas. The first, Tiberius, was well-meaning but was accused (albeit by hostile historians) of disgusting behaviour on Capri. The second, Gaius, nicknamed Caligula or 'little boot' as a child, proclaimed his sister a goddess and was unpredictable to the point of insanity. The third, Claudius, was considered decrepit but enjoyed an unexpected triumph (riding an elephant to mark the conquest of Britain); he was poisoned by his fourth wife, Agrippina, so that her son, Nero, could become emperor. Nero would have been happier on the stage and, after a disastrous reign, he killed himself.

From then on, imperial history was to be a succession of the good, the bad and, in the majority, the mediocre. Some emperors insisted on being treated as gods; almost all knew they needed to keep the army on their side. Constantine was the first Christian emperor, and by AD 393 the pagan cults, including emperor-worship, had been banned.

The unstable Nero (reigned AD 54–68) saw himself as Rome's first artist. His bizarre activities, murdering his mother and wife and appearing on stage, outraged respectable Roman opinion.

CITIZENS OF ROME

Roman society was stratified but not static. Patricians claimed family trees dating back to Rome's founders, while equites or knights were mostly businessmen who had become rich. The mass of the people were either free but poor, or slaves. To be a Roman citizen was a privilege reserved for Italians only, until AD 212 when Emperor Caracalla extended the privilege to all freemen, be they British, Libyan, Syrian or Spaniard.

Citizenship created a bond between Romans that was both valued and socially necessary. People stayed with friends, or friends of friends, when travelling, and young men looked to older men for advancement. Many men adopted sons, as well as having natural sons. Pliny the Younger (AD 61–113) was the adopted son of the polymath Pliny the Elder. The younger Pliny helped his old nurse move to a small farm, lent money to friends, and sent a servant on holiday for the sake of his health – acts regarded as highly proper for a Roman gentleman.

AN AFTERNOON AT THE THEATRE

Roman actors wore masks, coloured costumes and wigs to denote their characters – white for older men, black for young men, red for slaves. Plays often lasted for several hours, so audiences brought food and drink with them. They preferred comedies, noisily applauding good bits and hissing their disapproval.

A musical evening; the instrument shown in this fresco from a house in Pompeii is a lyre or kithara, a stringed instrument often played by singers while entertaining.

A portrait of Paquius Proculus and his wife, from the fresco in their home at Pompeii. He was evidently a prominent citizen, with one of the more elegant houses in the town, on the principal road.

A slave could rise to riches in Roman society. Ctesipus, a laundry-slave, was given as a 'free gift' to a wealthy Roman woman in a slave sale. He became her lover, she freed him and left him her fortune. When the orator Cicero's librarian slave, Tiro, became ill, Cicero freed him; Tiro recovered, wrote Cicero's biography, became a country gentleman and lived to be 100 years old.

Women played little part in public life, although some women wielded considerable influence in private. Soldiers' wives sometimes went along on foreign missions. Pompona Graecina accompanied her husband, Aulus Plautius, the general who led the Roman army that invaded Britain in AD 43.

Romans enjoyed seasonal festivals: a sowing festival in spring, a harvest festival and, in December, the seven-day Saturnalia in honour of Saturn, the god of agriculture, when schools and law courts closed for the feasting and masters served slaves. At home, Romans enjoyed music, stories and games. Children played marbles with nuts, and jacks with knucklebones. Robbers, a board game in which counters could be 'stolen' by your opponent, was a favourite of soldiers. Outdoor games included trigon, a ball-throwing game for three players, harpastum, which was a bit like rugby, and paganica, which seems to have been a free fight with a ball!

'I had a good win at dice – and did not cheat,' someone wrote on the wall of a bathhouse in Pompeii. Gambling games, using counters and dice like these, were especially popular in the Roman army.

TOWN AND COUNTRY LIVING

The quality of Roman life was exemplified by civic pride and duty. The Romans built civic centres with town halls, tax offices and public spaces. Almost every Roman town had a public bathhouse. At one time, there were more than 800 public baths in Rome, and the huge Baths of Diocletian held 3,000 people. Large villas had private bath suites, but when in town Romans liked to meet at the baths after lunch. On the way to the baths, a citizen might catch up with the news. Rome's newspaper, the *Acta Diurna* (Daily News), handwritten, was founded by Julius Caesar in 59 BC.

Country villas, ranging from the modest to the palatial, produced food, and every day carts trundled into town with grain, fruit, vegetables, meat and wine. Most poor Romans survived on a diet of bread and wheat porridge, but the better-off enjoyed dinner parties, at which the dishes ranged from ostrich brains to sliced eggs and mackerel served with parsley. The writer Martial lists marrows, lettuce, leeks, beans, mint and chicory on the menu for a dinner with friends, with a main course of lamb, chicken and the remains of the previous day's ham.

Daily bread was a must for most Romans. This stone relief shows a baker and a customer checking the loaves for freshness.

Plaster casts of victims of the disaster that struck Pompeii in August AD 79, when the volcano Vesuvius erupted and buried the seaside town in lava and ash.

A street in Pompeii. Typically a Roman town had two main roads (north–south, east–west) intersecting to create a grid. Pompeii had pedestrian crossings (raised stones) and a traffic system (judging by well-worn wheel ruts), but no street names.

Roman in a bikini. She is one of 10 young women shown exercising, in mosaic, on the walls of a room in the Villa Romana del Casale, Sicily. Dating from the 4th century AD, the mosaics may have been made by North African artists, judging by the origin of some of the materials used.

The Roman statesman and orator Cato (234–149 BC), regarded as the model citizen, warned his son against Greek doctors, who 'have sworn to kill all barbarians with their drugs'. Many doctors in the Empire were Greeks; they performed delicate operations, such as removing cataracts with needles. Asclepius, the Greek god of healing, had a temple on an island in the Tiber, and sick people spent the night there hoping for a cure.

Some treatments worked: the juice of poppy seeds could soothe crying babies and extract of willow bark (containing salicylic acid, or aspirin) brought down fevers. Prescriptions for baldness, including the fat of lions, hippos and crocodiles smeared on the head, were less useful. A brisk trade was done in love potions, and people cursed their enemies by scrawling bad luck messages on bits of pottery and tossing them into the river.

FISH SAUCE WITH EVERYTHING

The Romans were particularly fond of a fishy sauce known as liquamen or garum. The sauce was made from the gills, blood and guts of fish, marinated in a jar with whole small fish, salt, wine, herbs and vinegar. Left in the sun for two to three months, the contents became liquid, and highly aromatic! The sauce was bottled, labelled and sold. And apparently it was eaten with practically everything – from pears to veal. The Roman palate liked sweet and sour. The dregs left behind after fermentation of the sauce were made into a strongly flavoured paste, sold to the poor.

DEATH IN THE SAND

The image of Rome is, for many, the gladiator. Originating in the funeral games of the Etruscans, by the time of Augustus gladiator fights had become bloody spectacles staged by the emperor to win popularity with the public and impress foreign visitors.

The name gladiator comes from the Latin *gladius*, meaning a short sword. Many gladiators were prisoners of war, and names such as 'Samnite' or 'Thracian' reminded arena spectators of the gladiators' origins. Others were slaves and a few were volunteers. Gladiators were variously armed and armoured. Some fought on horseback, others in armour so heavy they could barely move. There were men with nets and tridents, men with lassos, men with swords – all trying to kill one another in front of a baying crowd.

Nero liked female gladiators and in AD 66 staged a battle between Ethiopian men, women and children to entertain a visiting king of Armenia. Emperor Domitian (AD 81–96) staged all-female fights at night by torchlight as well as contests between women and dwarfs.

Gladiators fighting, from a vase in the Colchester and Essex Museum, Colchester. Most gladiators died in the arena but some survived 30 or more contests into scarred retirement.

The Colosseum in Rome today. Wild beasts and condemned prisoners were brought up from beneath the sanded arena, now with its floor gone.

SLAVE REVOLT

A Thracian gladiator and ex-slave named Spartacus led an uprising in 73 BC. Spartacus and his army of 70,000 slaves and runaways were hunted by three Roman armies; they were eventually trapped in the far south of Italy by General Crassus in 71 BC, and Spartacus was killed. Over 6,000 of his followers were crucified along the Appian Way, the road from Capua to Rome.

A beast-fighter impales a leopard on his spear; from a mosaic of the 4th century AD.

Gladiators fought with a variety of weapons. This one holds a whip and a long hunting-style spear.

A beaten gladiator submitted by holding up his left index finger or by falling to his knees and reversing his sword. The referee appealed to the spectators. If the gladiator had fought well, he was spared; if the verdict was 'death', the gladiator offered his neck to the victor's sword. His body was lugged out by attendants dressed as demons from the underworld, the sand was raked over, and the show went on.

Gladiator fights were often preceded by wild animal shows. The Romans shipped in thousands of exotic creatures from Africa: elephants, rhinos, hippos, lions, leopards, giraffes, camels, wild asses, crocodiles and monkeys. There were tigers from Asia, bulls from Greece, bears and aurochs (wild oxen) from northern Europe. Animals were slaughtered by armed men, pitted against one another, or set upon criminals.

Crowds of up to 50,000 packed the Colosseum, Rome's largest amphitheatre. A netted barrier 5 metres (16 feet) high prevented animals from leaping into the seating. Beasts were caged beneath the arena and brought up in lifts, along with the scenery required to recreate a myth, such as Actaeon (played by a convict) being torn to pieces by the goddess Diana's hounds.

ROMAN VIRTUES

Hard work, thrift, honesty, patience, endurance, courage, simplicity …
the qualities of a farmer and soldier. It was these virtues that the citizens
of Rome most admired.

Roman virtues were nurtured within the family. Fathers had power of
life and death over wives, children, servants and slaves. Women were often
expected to be 'silent partners', looking after the home and children, always
loyal to their husbands. To be unmarried was a social and economic disaster
for most women.

Romans chose their wedding day with care, to avoid the many
'ill-omened' days in the calendar. The second half of June brought a rush of
weddings. Helpers did the bride's hair using an iron spearhead to shape the
locks into a cone, held together by ribbons. Her veil and shoes were flame-
orange, her white dress fastened at the waist with a belt tied in a special knot.

D·M·C·IVL·MATERNV

*A family meal, from the
3rd century AD, with people
seated on chairs rather than
reclining on couches as at an
upper-class dinner party.
Father is the dominant
figure. Romans believed
personal spirits watched over
each child, to adulthood. For
a woman, to be childless
could mean a bleak future.*

*Portrait of a young woman
from a fresco at Pompeii.
Thoughtfully holding her
stylus-pen and wax tablet,
she is said to represent the
Greek poet Sappho.*

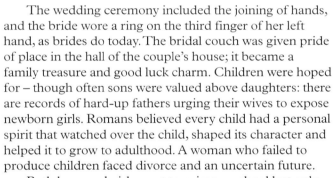

A household shrine, from the House of the Vettii, a well-to-do home in Pompeii. Two household gods dance either side of the owner; the snake symbolizes his Genius or guardian spirit.

This bronze figure of a Lar, or house-spirit, would have stood on a household altar.

The wedding ceremony included the joining of hands, and the bride wore a ring on the third finger of her left hand, as brides do today. The bridal couch was given pride of place in the hall of the couple's house; it became a family treasure and good luck charm. Children were hoped for – though often sons were valued above daughters: there are records of hard-up fathers urging their wives to expose newborn girls. Romans believed every child had a personal spirit that watched over the child, shaped its character and helped it to grow to adulthood. A woman who failed to produce children faced divorce and an uncertain future.

Both boys and girls went to primary school but only well-off families educated girls beyond the basics. Some taught their sons at home, often with a slave tutor. The historian Plutarch tells us that Cato taught his son reading, writing, law, gymnastics, horse riding, boxing, swimming and how to stand up to heat and cold: even to a Roman, this was a somewhat old-fashioned upbringing. Later Roman boys learned Greek and Latin literature, history, arithmetic, geometry and astronomy.

Fifty was a good age for a Roman man, although women were vulnerable to earlier death through childbearing. A Roman funeral, normally held at night, was led by musicians playing trumpets. After much weeping and a eulogy, the body was either burned or buried.

POWER OF THE UNSEEN

Romans believed every action was shaped by unseen powers. Houses had shrines to the household gods: Vesta, spirit of hearth and fire; Penates, who looked after the store-cupboard; and Lares, who watched over households. Each family had one protective Lar, usually shown in small statues as a curly headed youth, dancing. Above his head the Lar raises a *rhyton* (drinking cup) from which wine flows into a *patera* (a round dish, for libations or sacrificial offerings). He was invoked for all family events, such as a marriage. Every day, fathers made offerings of food, milk and wine to the household gods, and said prayers.

GODS AND THE AFTERLIFE

Romans honoured their ancestors but also feared the dead as hostile spirits to be warded off by rite and prayer. Their religion had more to do with life than death, for deities controlled various spheres of life. Many were Roman versions of the Greek Olympians. The Roman gods were led by the sky god Jupiter, whose wife was Juno. Other 'great gods' were Vesta, Minerva, Ceres, Diana, Venus, Mars, Mercury, Neptune, Vulcan and Apollo. And there were many lesser ones, including nymphs, fauns, mermen and other nature spirits. There was even a deity for the house-proud: Deverra, spirit of the broom.

People went to temples to seek help or advice and to make offerings (food, money, flowers or a small statue). Roman priests were elected and belonged to 'colleges'; the chief college was that of the pontifices, guardians of sacred law. Priests performed public rituals, such as sacrificing a chicken or a bull. The entrails of animals provided soothsayers with answers to questions about the future, while other omens were interpreted by the augurs, gazing at the flight of birds.

A coin showing the two-headed god Janus, god of doors and gateways, who knew both past and future. January is named after him.

Statue of Jupiter, king of gods and serial parent, in the Vatican Museum, Rome. He was the most powerful and most feared of all Roman gods.

The Romans were usually tolerant of foreign religious notions and adopted gods from all over the Empire. The emperor was expected to honour the ancient gods (Jupiter and the others), but might also venerate household spirits, deified emperors and others – Severus Alexander (reigned AD 222–235) made space in his chapel for Orpheus, Abraham and Christ. A favourite with the Roman army was Mithras, a warrior god of Persian (Iranian) origin, admired as a guardian of law and truth. Mithraism for a time rivalled Christianity as the new imperial faith.

Pagan Romans believed the dead went to the underworld, ruled by Pluto. Pluto's world was not heaven or hell: it was more like an infinity of wet days. To many Romans in the 1st century AD, Christianity offered a more tempting prospect. Christians, like Jews, were persecuted because they refused to pay lip service to the gods of Rome and to the emperor, which was treason. Persecution began under Nero (who blamed Christians for setting fire to Rome) and ended, violently, under Diocletian in the period AD 303–311. Under Emperor Constantine, 20 years later, Christians found themselves free from fear and in favour. The pagan temples were emptied of their treasures. Churches, not temples, were now in vogue.

A bust of Serapis, an Egyptian underworld god, unearthed in London in 1954 and now in the Museum of London. The Romans adopted foreign deities readily, perhaps thinking that each new god provided a little more assurance in an uncertain world.

Play-figures, from a British-Roman child's grave found at Colchester. They came from a toy dinner party, which included guests and servants, as well as couches and chairs on which the child could arrange the figures.

THE STORY OF PROSERPINA

The Romans borrowed many myths from the Greeks, among them the story of Persephone, who became Proserpina in the Roman version. The god Pluto carried her off to the underworld. When he refused to release her, her mother, the cereal goddess Ceres, conjured a terrible drought. The harvest withered and to save mankind from starvation, Jupiter ruled that Proserpina must live above ground for six months and return to the underworld for the rest of the year. Thus, the bright days of summer became the gloom of winter.

ROMAN STYLE

Most of what we know about Roman houses comes from archaeological finds such as those at Pompeii and Herculaneum, and at Ostia, Rome's port at the mouth of the Tiber. Notable British sites include the palace at Fishbourne in West Sussex. Houses were built of brick and stone or (later) of concrete, and roofed with tiles. The central atrium or main hall was open to the weather, letting in light and rainwater which collected in a central pool.

Large houses were warmed by furnaces circulating hot air in the spaces within walls and under floors; smaller ones by fires burning in iron braziers or stone hearths. Interior decoration included wall paintings and floor mosaics, made from small cubes, called tesserae, made of stone, tiles, glass and pottery. Roman plumbers used lead or ceramic pipes, but no taps. Water flowed continuously through bathhouses and public toilets, in which users sat in a row over a channel of running water.

Romans liked jewellery. This earring (1st century AD) is made of gold set with semi-precious stones; now in the British Museum, London.

Fishbourne Roman Palace, a model of the palatial residence that originally had 100 rooms with mosaic floors. The palace may have been home to the provincial governor or to a local British chieftain, Cogidubnus, an ally of the Roman invaders in the 1st century AD.

Sandals were the standard footwear for Romans, men and women.

Romans drank wines described as 'black, red, white or yellow'. To drink neat wine was regarded as uncouth: water was added and some-times honey. Grapes and olives were the two most important crops after cereals. Olive oil production was enormous: one rubbish dump found near Rome contained 40 million pots used for oil.

Servants prepared food in the kitchen and carried it to the dining room, where guests reclined on couches. Slaves brought finger bowls and towels for guests, who were expected to bring their own napkins.

Dressing for dinner could take hours. The desired pale complexion was achieved with powdered chalk or white lead. Red ochre brought a blush to cheeks and lips. Slaves and mistresses together lavished much care on the hair. At times, it was fashionable to dye hair blonde or red, or to wear wigs. Pumice stone removed hair from the legs and depilatory creams included such unlikely substances as wild goat's blood and powdered snake. Tooth powder was made from cow's horn, burnt oyster shell and the ashes of a dog's teeth.

A Roman mirror, found at Wroxeter in Shropshire, one of the chief towns in Roman Britain.

The toga, most Roman of costumes, was worn only by Roman citizens. The semicircular piece of cloth (usually wool or linen, but silk for the ultra-rich) was loose and comfortable, but not easy to wear in informal situations. Tunics, for men and women, were more functional. In cold weather, cloaks kept out wind and rain, while a man might cover his legs with ankle-length tight trousers. Feet were shod in sandals or leather boots, with knitted wool socks or woven cloth stockings for extra warmth.

A Roman beauty, thought to be Poppaea Sabina. Twice-married, she cap-tivated Nero and, it was rumoured, encouraged him to get rid of both his mother and wife.

19

LEGIONS OF IRON

The Roman army won, guarded and built the Empire. The backbone of the army was the legion, with a nominal strength of 5,500 to 6,000 men, although often it had fewer. The cohort was the equivalent of a battalion, and each legion had 10 cohorts: the first with 960 men and 9 others with 480 men. A century (originally 100 men, but 80 in the imperial army) was commanded by a centurion, usually promoted from the ranks. Field armies were normally commanded by consuls, the highest officials in Rome after the emperor.

Most of the legionaries were infantry soldiers and all were Roman citizens. In imperial times most were recruited from outside Italy. The minimum joining age was 20. The men were well paid, rigorously trained and pensioned off to veterans' settlements after 25 years, if they survived. Auxiliaries were non-citizens, recruited from around the Empire. They fought in the front line, being expendable, and were paid less than a legionary, but from the 1st century AD were granted Roman citizenship on discharge.

The campaign season began in March and lasted until October, when the legions went into winter quarters. In battles, armies often became locked together, lines of men

Probably the oldest Roman gravestone in Britain shows a cavalryman crushing British resistance. A Bulgarian named Longinus Sdapeze, he died at Colchester in AD 49, after serving for 15 years, so he probably landed with the Roman invasion army of AD 43.

heaving and straining for advantage. Cavalry might surge across the field, and harry fleeing enemies, but it was the infantry who most often won the day. They advanced in lines, to the sound of javelins clashing on shields and braying trumpets. Nearing the enemy, the men flung their javelins (each soldier carried two). The long spear bent on impact, so it could not be hurled back, and in the confusion the Roman infantry charged, stabbing with swords from behind their shields, the front line pressed forward by the weight of those behind.

Legions fought desperately to save their eagle standard from capture. To lose an eagle was a deep disgrace. A unit found guilty of mutiny or cowardice was 'decimated'. One man in 10 was chosen for death, often by being beaten to death by his comrades.

The imperial 'household guard' was the Praetorian Guard, based in Rome. They protected, and sometimes helped to remove, emperors, until disbanded by Constantine in AD 312.

Tombstone of Marcus Favonius Facilis, a centurion of the 20th Legion in Britain. He carries a vine staff (symbol of his power to flog troopers) and has a sword (on the left) and a dagger. He died at Colchester before AD 60; his cremated bones were found beneath his stone.

Remains of the legionary fortress at Caerleon, South Wales. Each barrack block housed 80 men.

ROMAN WEAPONS

Romans wore two types of armour: *lorica segmentata*, made from metal strips or *lorica hamata*, chain mail. A soldier's main weapons were his javelin (*pilum*) and sword (*gladius*), and he protected himself with a curved shield (*scutum*). Other weapons deployed by the army included slingshots, bows and arrows, and artillery such as the stone-throwing *ballista* and the bolt-firing *scorpion*.

A dagger, from Pompeii, and a Roman soldier's scabbard, recovered from the River Thames in London. The scabbard was probably lost during Boudicca's attack on the city in AD 60 or 61.

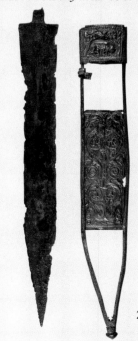

EMPIRE OF DIVERSITY

The Romans regarded most non-Romans as 'barbarians' – even when highly civilized (like the Persians or Egyptians). To be Roman was to be a member of a select, if increasingly large, club. But as their empire grew to a vast size, they became more accustomed to dealing with a host of different peoples. The frontier still had to be guarded – to keep out unwelcome intruders such as German tribes straying across the Rhine – but by and large the Roman Empire managed diversity issues fairly well.

The Pont du Gard is a Roman aqueduct near Nîmes, in southern France. Constructed in AD 19, it has three tiers rising to a height of 48 metres (157 feet).

Communication was the key to running such a diverse empire. Most trade was carried on by private traders, although the state controlled shipments of corn and metal. Rome's biggest cargo ships carried grain and could also transport up to 600 people. Barges carried freight along rivers and canals. To protect this commerce from pirates, the Roman fleet patrolled the ocean. Its biggest ships were 45 metres (150 feet) long, crewed by 572 oarsmen, 30 sailors and 250 marines. Rome relied on grain imports from North Africa and, in the 1st century AD, 200,000 people in Rome were registered for a free food handout. No emperor felt safe when there were food riots.

A marble head of Medusa, from the Roman city of Leptis Magna in Libya. During the reign of Septimus Severus (AD 193– 211), who was born there, Leptis Magna became one of the most splendid cities in the Roman Empire.

AS THE ROMANS
SAW THINGS

Julius Caesar, in his *Gallic Wars*, gives a brisk, soldierly account of his two campaigns in Britain: '… the Britons call a stronghold any densely wooded spot fortified by a rampart and ditch …', but after a dozen pages or so returns to his main thesis, the wars in Gaul and his own qualities as leader. Roman historians seldom passed judgements without bias. The historian Tacitus (AD 55–118) is a prime source for Roman Britain. But he leaves out much local colour that we would love to know. Instead he mocks the British for adopting Roman ways so slavishly. He married the daughter of General Agricola, whom he lavishly praises, but he never mentions his wife's name.

The amphitheatre at El Djem in Tunisia, second in size only to the Colosseum in Rome.

Getting around the Empire was uncomfortable by road and slow by sea. Most ships kept close to the coast so even a short journey took days. Shipwrecks were an expected hazard. It was slightly safer to walk, ride or sit in a wagon, but most travellers kept together in groups. A rich Roman woman about town might be carried in a litter by her slaves.

The Romans were assiduous writers of letters. For short letters and notes they used wax tablets; for longer writings they used pen (reed or goose-feather) and ink on papyrus. The imperial post was for official letters only. Couriers changed horses at way stations every 10–15 kilometres (6–10 miles). It was a capital offence to interfere with the couriers or the documents they carried. Private citizens sent letters by a slave or asked a friend who was going in the right direction; it was also quite usual to ask a stranger to take a letter. The fastest way was to ask a courier employed by the tax office to add your letter to his bag; in this way a letter from Britain might reach Rome in 30 days.

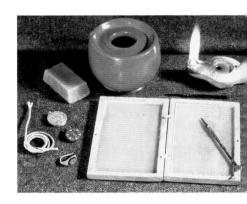

Roman writing materials, including an ink-pot, a seal ring and an oil lamp; from the Verulamium Museum, St Albans, Hertfordshire.

IMMORTAL PANTHEON

Immortality was conferred by great deeds, widely reported. Most of the 'great' Romans came from the ruling classes: aristocrats, generals, consuls, senators, emperors good and ghastly. They became the stars of Roman history and of dramas, from Shakespeare to Hollywood: Julius Caesar, Mark Antony, Nero, Hadrian, Marcus Aurelius, Constantine, Cicero. Few women had such prominent roles. There were notorious courtesans, such as Messalina, the third wife of Emperor Claudius, who was put to death in AD 48 for plotting to overthrow her husband. But there were female examples of virtue and achievement, too, such as Hortensia, who spoke out against harsh tax laws imposed on women in the 40s BC, and Hypatia, whose brilliance as a scientist attracted students to Alexandria, until she was killed in AD 415 by a mob who believed her to be a magician.

Virgil (Publius Vergilius Maro, 70−19 BC), the greatest Roman poet, is shown with two of the Muses in this 3rd-century mosaic from Sousse in Tunisia.

Republican idealist Marcus Tullius Cicero (106−43 BC) was Rome's most famous lawyer-orator. He fatally underestimated Octavian (Augustus) after the assassination of Julius Caesar in 44 BC, remarking that 'the young man should be given praise, distinctions − and then be disposed of'. Soon afterwards Cicero was captured and put to death on Octavian's orders.

Not all great Romans were high-born. Terence (*c.*190–159 BC), one of Rome's most famous play-wrights, was born in Carthage and taken as a slave to Rome by a senator who named him, educated him and freed him. The poet Horace (65–8 BC) was the son of a freed slave, but through his writing earned a country house and a state stipend. Above all other Roman writers towers Virgil (70–19 BC), son of a well-to-do farmer and author of the *Aeneid*, the epic poem about the adventures of Aeneas after the siege of Troy.

Pliny the Younger perhaps shows us his ideal Roman when writing about a retired governor named Spurinna whose routine, aged 77, he admiringly records in a letter. He writes that Spurinna wakes at dawn, lies in for an hour, walks three miles, has a book read to him, talks with friends while out for a drive, has another walk, writes some poetry, sunbathes, exercises briskly with a ball, then has a bath, followed by a rest, dinner and more talk or a play until the stars appear. Perhaps only Pliny's uncle, Pliny the Elder, was more admirable – with his 20 books on the German wars and his 37 volumes on natural history!

Roman dignity: a head of Hadrian, found in the River Thames near London Bridge in 1834. It probably comes from a statue erected in honour of the emperor's visit to Britain in AD 122.

Hadrian's Wall, 117 kilometres (73 miles) long, was built in six years (AD 122–128). The wall controlled the frontier between the province of Britannia and non-Roman Britain. It is now a UNESCO World Heritage Site.

WAREHOUSE OF THE WORLD

Roman civilization could appear ostentatious, yet its art and technology were basically utilitarian. The Romans imitated 'classical' styles, principally Greek, but also pioneered innovations such as the vault, arch and dome. No dome to match that of the Pantheon in Rome was built until modern times. Intensely practical, the Romans built walls, baths, aqueducts, central heating systems and harbours. They built roads better than any others in the ancient world. The roads enabled them to move troops quickly and they also facilitated trade between the cities the Romans built wherever they went.

A Roman forge, shown in a 2nd-century relief. The Romans made high-quality iron and experimented with steel.

Roman amphorae (large pottery jars) were all-purpose containers. These, from Turkey, are stacked as they would have been in the hold of a ship.

Earrings in the form of doves, a gold medallion showing the love-goddess Aphrodite, and an ornate gold ring, all from the 1st century BC and now in the British Museum, London.

A mosaic from Ostia, Rome's port, shows a cargo vessel (right) and a naval galley, with a friendly dolphin.

Roman technology was simple but very effective. The Romans had few machines, relying heavily on slaves and animals. Donkeys turned millstones and oxen and horses pulled carts. In the 1st century BC, Vitruvius invented a water mill: one in Gaul (France) drove 16 mills, grinding enough grain to feed 12,000 people a day. The Romans also invented a reaping machine, the *vallus*. It was pushed by a donkey and had prongs to cut shear the stalks and a hopper to collect the grain. But it was not widely used: farms had plenty of slaves.

Writing in the 2nd century AD, Aelius Aristides, described Rome as the 'the world's warehouse'. Imperial trade and diplomatic contacts reached India and even China. At its peak in about AD 100, a million people lived in Rome, making it the biggest city in the world. Yet the edifice could not last. By the time the last Western Roman emperor, Romulus Augustulus, was removed in 476, there were only 100,000 people living in Rome. The grandeur had crumbled, yet the idea and the ideals of Rome lived on.

Two examples of Roman glassware (from the 1st century AD), with 'splash' decoration, each about 13 centimetres (5 inches) high.

SMART THINKING

The Romans seldom admitted that a problem could not be solved. When in 52 BC Julius Caesar was caught between two armies of Gauls, he set about an astonishing feat of military engineering. He constructed a series of walls and ditches to keep the Gauls in Alesia hemmed in. He then constructed another wall to keep the Gallic reinforcements at bay, enclosing his army between the inner and outer rings of fortifications. This 'double circumvallation' included 23 forts, a trench 6 metres (20 feet) wide, earth ramparts with towers, and trenches booby-trapped with pointed stakes and iron spikes. In all, the earthworks extended for 40 kilometres (25 miles). Out-dug, the Gauls surrendered.

Roman Heritage

The Roman Empire left an enduring legacy, even in outposts such as Britain, where its monuments include Hadrian's Wall, the baths at Bath (Aquae Sulis) and the remains of the legionary bases at Caerleon and Chester. There are the remains of shore forts (Pevensey), Roman cities (Silchester, Wroxeter, York, London) and villas (Fishbourne, Chedworth). Museums across Europe display Roman relics, from armour to leather shoes. Roman battles are re-enacted by enthusiasts dressed as legionaries, and television shows bring Roman history and archaeology into the sitting room.

While Roman buildings crumbled, the idea of the Roman Empire was sustained. Rulers such as Charlemagne in the 800s and Napoleon a thousand years later dreamed in Roman terms, while the Holy Roman Empire, centred on Germany, lasted from 962 until 1806. Precious vestiges of Roman learning were preserved by scholars in both East and West, to be 'rediscovered' during the European Renaissance of the 1400s–1500s. The Catholic Church in Rome used Latin in its liturgy, and Latin literature influenced many writers – John Milton, for example. The Latin language was read and written by scholars and scientists, too, long after it had ceased to be spoken. The calendar, numerals, the law, even the ways towns were planned: all bore the Roman stamp.

Roman architectural style became newly fashionable first in Italy then throughout Europe, with the classical revival in England completely triumphant by the 18th century. In the 19th century, statues of great men in London squares were even dressed in togas. By then, many Victorians saw themselves as latter-day Romans. Unlike the ghost in Pliny's story (see panel), the Romans have never quite gone away.

A room at Kedleston Hall, Derbyshire, an example of 1760s neo-classical style by Robert Adam. Adam modelled the south front of the Curzon family home on the Arch of Constantine in Rome.

A Roman ghost story

Pliny the Younger tells a ghost story about a haunted house. Athenodorus, a philosopher, took the house at a giveaway price. The ghost, an old man rattling chains, appeared before Athenodorus, and beckoned him to follow him. In the courtyard, the ghost vanished. Athenodorus ordered a hole to be dug and a skeleton in chains was unearthed. Given proper burial, the spirit departed and the philosopher could enjoy his house in peace.

The Byzantine Empress Theodora (AD 500–548), with attendants; from a mosaic in the Church of San Vitale, Ravenna, Italy. The daughter of a 'bear keeper' in Constantinople, this remarkable woman became wife and adviser to the Emperor Justinian.

Front cover: Stone head of Emperor Augustus, crowned with an oak wreath.
Back cover: Bronze head of the goddess Sulis Minerva; now in the Roman Baths Museum, Bath.

Acknowledgements
Photographs are reproduced by kind permission of the following: Alamy: 1t (Adam Eastland), 1bl (Bildarchiv Monheim GmbH), 1br (Ian M Butterfield), 2/3 (Tibor Bognar), 4t (Mary Evans), 4b (Gary Cook), 6l (North Wind Picture Library), 6r, 7br, 16tr (Visual Arts Library), 10br (Ace Stock Ltd), 11tl (Anthony Ibarra), 12b (Pixonneet.com), 16b (Brian Atkinson), 20/21 (Richard Naude), 22bl (T S Corrigon), 23 (Eye Ubiquitous), 25b (Robert Harding Picture Library), 26tr (David Kilpatrick), 27t (AA World Travel Library), 28t (National Trust Photolibrary); Ancient Art & Architecture Collection: 21tr; Art Archive: 2; Bridgeman Art Library: FC, 19b (Louvre, Paris, France), 3 (Museo Capitolino, Rome, Italy), 5bl, (Roger-Viollet, Paris Museo della Civilta, Rome, Italy), 5br, 14l (Museo e Gallerie Nazionali di Capodimonte, Naples, Italy), 7t, 8 both (Museo Archaeologico Nazionale, Naples, Italy), 9t (Bildarchiv Steffens, Rheinisches Landesmuseum, Bonn, Germany), 9b (Musee Alesia, Alise-Sainte-Reine, France), 10cl, 13b, 14cr, 26cl (Museo della Civilta Romana, Rome, Italy), 11tr (Villa Romana del Casale, Piazza Americana, Sicily), 13t (Alinari, Galleria Borghese, Rome, Italy), 15tl (Alinari, Pompeii, Italy), 15tr, 27b (Ashmolean Museum), 17tr (Museum of London), 18tr, 26b (British Museum), 23b (Verulamium Museum, St Albans), 24cl (Musee National du Bardo, Le Bardo, Tunisia), 24br (Alinari Galleria degli Uffizi, Florence, Italy), 28b (San Vitale, Ravenna, Italy); Colchester Museum: 12cr, 17bl, 20tl, 21cl; Pont du Gard: 22tr; Pitkin Publishing Ltd: BC; Shrewsbury Museum: 19cr; Sussex Past: 18b; TopFoto: 19tl, 21br (British Museum/HIP), 25cl (Museum of London/HIP).

Written by Brian Williams; the author has asserted his moral rights.
Edited by Clare Collinson.
Designed by Simon Borrough.
Picture research by Jan Kean.
Map by The Map Studio Ltd, Romsey, Hants, UK.
The publishers would like to thank John Rhodes and Julie Hurst for reading the text.

Printed in Great Britain.
ISBN: 978 1 84165 202 3   1/07

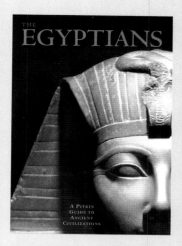

PITKIN GUIDES TO ANCIENT CIVILIZATIONS

This guide is just one in a series of history titles
Available by mail order
See our website,
www.jarrold-publishing.co.uk,
for our full range of titles, or contact us for a copy of our brochure

Pitkin Publishing Ltd, Healey House, Dene Road, Andover, Hampshire, SP10 2AA, UK
Enquiries: 01264 409200
Fax: 01264 334110
Sales: 01453 883300
Sales Fax: 01453 883233
Email: sales@tempus-publishing.com

PITKIN

ISBN 978-1-84165-202-3

9 781841 652023